Fear of Crowds

A Guide to Overcoming the Fear of Crowds in 6 Easy Steps

by Anila Sepp

Table of Contents

Introduction 1

Step 1: Logically Evaluating Your Condition 7

Step 2: Utilizing Relaxation Techniques 11

Step 3: Cultivating Social Skills 15

Step 4: Gaining Confidence through Scripting 19

Step 5: Keeping a Diary 23

Step 6: Seeking Professional Help 27

Conclusion 35

Introduction

The fear of crowds is a very real condition that thousands of people in the world suffer from. Enochlophobia, a condition wherein a person experiences an intense fear of large groups of people, is also often referred to as demophobia or ochlophobia. This fear can be so powerful that it has actually prevented people from going out of their homes, traveling, socializing with other people, and in short, living normal lives. This is the reason why any person suffering from this socially impairing condition should actively search for the way to bravely overcome it so that he or she can finally be able to rejoin society and function normally in it. I certainly hope that's why you're here reading this now.

Overcoming demophobia, enochlophobia, or ochlophobia is quite possible, especially if you have a real desire to be free of such a controlling disorder. By this, I mean that you must be willing to try all possible treatments and if necessary, even seek professional help in order to be rid of this phobia.

In this book, I'm going to describe a very straightforward path that anyone who is afflicted with this fear should try *before* having to go the route of seeking professional help. This book is geared to help you overcome enochlophobia in simple and easy steps, allowing you to take back full control of your life. Let's get started!

© Copyright 2015 by Miafn LLC - All rights reserved.

This document is geared towards providing reliable information in regards to the topic and issue covered. The publication is sold with the idea that the publisher is not required to render accounting, officially permitted, or otherwise, qualified services. If advice is necessary, legal or professional, a practiced individual in the profession should be ordered.

- From a Declaration of Principles which was accepted and approved equally by a Committee of the American Bar Association and a Committee of Publishers and Associations.

In no way is it legal to reproduce, duplicate, or transmit any part of this document in either electronic means or in printed format. Recording of this publication is strictly prohibited and any storage of this document is not allowed unless with written permission from the publisher. All rights reserved.

The information provided herein is stated to be truthful and consistent, in that any liability, in terms of inattention or otherwise, by any usage or abuse of any policies, processes, or directions contained within is solely and completely the responsibility of the recipient reader. Under no circumstances will any legal responsibility or blame be held against the publisher for any reparation, damages, or monetary loss due to the information herein, either directly or indirectly.

Respective authors own all copyrights not held by the publisher.

The information herein is offered for informational purposes solely, and is universal as so. The presentation of the information is without contract or any type of guarantee assurance.

The trademarks that are used are without any consent, and the publication of the trademark is without permission or backing by the trademark owner. All trademarks and brands within this book are for clarifying purposes only and are the owned by the owners themselves, not affiliated with this document.

Step 1: Logically Evaluating Your Condition

Fear of crowds can stem from two causes: a false perception of danger and social anxiety. The person suffering from this kind of disorder may feel sudden attacks of panic when in the presence of a large group of people. For people afflicted with this condition it is quite possible to get caught in a stampede from which escaping to a safe place might be physically impossible, with all the people around. Individuals who have enochlophobia experience an intense discomfort at the sight and sound of many people, making it physically, emotionally, and mentally impossible for them to stay in a crowded place. Social anxiety also plays a big role in the development of enochlophobia. When a person has an unreasonable fear that he might be the topic of people's conversation and the target of their judgments and criticism, he could become anxious of crowds.

It's worth mentioning that encochlophobia, just like all other kinds of phobias, is an irrational fear. The anxiety that a person feels in the case of a phobia is, more often than not, unreasonable, unfounded, or illogical. The gravity of the anxiety and discomfort brought on by enochlophobia can vary for each person. An individual may suffer from a severe fear of crowds and he might never venture out of the confines of his home. He will arrange that all necessities for his survival be delivered to his door. On the other hand, some people may have a more manageable condition wherein they can be in a crowded place and control their anxiety but only when a family member (a person that they trust) is with them. Let's also not forget that the root causes of the development of enochlophobia for each person are different.

A person who has a severe condition of enochlophobia will greatly benefit from the help of a therapist. However, in cases where the fear is mild to manageable, the person can still try to do some things to help himself overcome this irrational fear.

Among the things that can be done to manage and finally overcome fear of crowds is self-analysis. Applying logic in every situation can do a great deal to prevent the onset of panic attacks. Try this the next time you start feeling anxious while in a crowded place: As you experience any discomfort or any signs of anxiety rising up within you, stop it on its tracks by telling yourself to stay calm. The next thing to do is to evaluate the situation logically. Look around you and understand what it is that can be causing your discomfort. Do you feel that there could be real danger while you are in that place? Why do you feel this way? Look at each person around you. They are minding their own business and may not even be paying attention to you. Are you afraid that you can get trapped between all these people? Why would that happen? It would also help to soothe your mind if you knew where the exits are in that area. Perhaps, you can try sitting near these exit points to help you deal with any feelings of possible danger. Nevertheless, the point in this exercise is to appease your mind that there is no impending danger that will fall upon you while you are in that place. By looking at your surroundings calmly and analyzing situations logically you can keep panic attacks at bay.

Step 2: Utilizing Relaxation Techniques

A highly effective way to keep your anxiety in control whenever you are in a crowded place is to practice relaxation techniques. You can relax your body and mind by doing some techniques. At any time you feel panic attacks rising, when you are at the grocery, in a subway train, at a concert, or at your kid's school, follow these useful steps:

Do Breathing Exercises

Whenever you feel anxiety building up, take deep breaths. Inhale deeply and exhale slowly. Repeat this as many times as you need to. Pay special attention to the rhythm of your breathing. Close your eyes if you need to and concentrate on the sound of your breath coming in and going out.

Calm Your Mind

The mind is a very powerful force. Luckily, you can control your mind. So don't help anxiety build up by feeding your mind with thoughts of imminent danger.

Instead, calm your mind. Repeat this chant in your head: "I am safe. I am not in danger. I am in a good place."

Refocus Your Attention

This technique instructs you to choose one thing pleasant to focus on. It can be a person, a décor in that place, or a memory in your mind. Focusing on something pleasant when you feel the panic attacks emerging can help you return to a peaceful state of mind. For instance, if you are at a party, it helps to concentrate your attention to one person only, perhaps your companion at this party, instead of paying attention to all the people around you.

Placing all of your attention to one thing allows you to block out all other stimuli around you. People with enochlophobia often feel mild discomfort to severe panic attacks at the idea of a crowd overpowering them. They feel that the noise made by large groups of people can prevent their voices from being heard and that they can easily get engulfed by a crowd. So when you focus on a single stimulus when you are in a crowded place, you don't give much attention to all the other people around you. You can block out their voices, smell, and movement. If you are in a subway, where strangers are almost always in close quarters, listening to music on your headphones can help you focus your attention. Concentrate on the music and not on the people around you.

There are numerous relaxation techniques you can try, starting from breathing exercises to refocusing your attention. People who practice yoga find they have the ability to stay calmer in situations that would have been normally agitating for most people. So find the relaxation technique that suits you best and use this as a coping mechanism when you feel anxious while in a crowded place. These relaxation techniques will greatly help anyone suffering from enochlophobia and allow them to live in close proximities with people in our society.

Step 3: Cultivating Social Skills

One of the possible causes of enochlophobia is social anxiety. When people fear what others will say about them, if they worry too much about not being socially accepted or even being judged or criticized, then they develop social anxiety. Fear of public speaking, a form of social anxiety, is also closely related to fear of crowds.

To some extent, many people develop a fear of crowds because they have social anxiety. They may have had some unpleasant experience on certain occasions when they were speaking in front of people or have had some unkind encounter with a large group of people. In some cases, individuals develop enochlophobia due to the lack of social skills. They are afraid that they wouldn't know what to say, how to respond, and how to have conversations with people. They feel some kind of pressure and discomfort during their social interactions.

To remedy this situation, a person who has enochlophobia can take a class where he can learn about social skills. Many folks suffering from fear of crowds will feel very nervous and sweat profusely. In addition, they can even experience various physical discomforts such as a headache, stomach pain, and possibly lose consciousness at the prospect of facing a crowd. One way to combat social anxiety and, at the same time, overcome enochlophobia is to learn skills that can help the phobic deal with people.

In a class that teaches social skills, the person can learn how to have simple conversations. They will be taught how to start a dialogue, make small talk, and learn possible responses to other people's inquiries. This is because, although the phobic knows how to respond to daily conversations, the fear of making a mistake, being criticized or judged will inhibit him from making the right responses. Therefore, a social skills class will review and reinforce all the proper social etiquette for interacting with other people. The class can also provide opportunities where the phobic person can "practice" socializing either with people from the class, with other instructors, or people from outside the class. The main purpose of learning social skills, whether for the first time or for reinforcement, is to build the confidence of the individuals suffering from social anxiety and the fear of crowds. If they know what is proper to say and do when socializing, the anxiety they normally feel when talking, mingling, or interacting with other people, can be decreased.

Step 4: Gaining Confidence through Scripting

The fear of crowds is not innate. It is typically acquired as a response to undesirable experiences. A person who was once very sociable and has loads of confidence can suddenly dread facing the public just because of a traumatic social event. It is not unusual for people suffering from enochlophobia to stutter, shake, and become incoherent when interacting with a group of people. They may lose the ability to respond to simple questions such as "Where are you heading?" and "What's that you're reading?"

Scripting is one of the methods to overcome fear of crowds. The coping mechanism involves writing down all possible responses to questions that other people might ask you. In the privacy of his home before he goes out, the person who is suffering from enochlophobia can prepare a script of answers to queries that people may ask him. Then, depending on the purpose for going out, the script could include information such as his name, address, medical records, and so on. Let's take a look at this example: Individuals with a fear of crowds may have a hard time going inside a grocery store to buy necessary supplies. So if a person suffering from enochlophobia went food shopping, he would have to prepare a script for the possible questions the cashier might ask and the answers that he could give in response. The cashier might ask a senior citizen whether he has identification cards and other proof of his age. He can also be asked if he has a smaller bill than the one he gave. All of these possible questions should be included in the script so that the phobic person can provide all the proper responses without panicking or feeling anxious during the social interaction.

Scripting has been proven to abate the occurrence of panic attacks in people suffering from social anxiety. It can also help control and finally overcome the fear of crowds.

Step 5: Keeping a Diary

Writing down all your thoughts and feelings throughout the day can empower you to overcome your fear. A journal lets you express yourself without reservations, and going back to read old entries gives insight to how you react to life's events and other patterns in your behavior. The whole process can take a long time and, at first, it may seem to produce no effect, still putting thoughts and feelings down on paper can prove to be beneficial in the long run.

Let's say that you have a doctor's appointment today but you were not able to keep it because of your fear of crowds. Going to the doctor's office would have required you to walk to the subway station, ride the train, get a cab to the doctor's office, talk to the receptionist, and wait in the lobby for a certain period with all the other patients. In your diary, write down how you feel about all this. Why did you cancel your appointment? What part of your trip to the clinic would have been the most uncomfortable for you had you chosen to keep your appointment? What part of the trip would have been the least uncomfortable? Why would any of these make you uncomfortable in the first place? If you write all of these down in detail, you will be able to see in writing your feelings and emotions. You can review this information and compare it with the input from the other days.

Keeping a diary will not only let you identify the possible triggers of your fear of crowds, but you will also know what situations are okay with you and what situations make you feel the most anxious. Once you identify the triggers of your enochlophobia, you will be able to rationalize it. What is it that bothers you so much about a crowd? Why does it bother you so much? Is there something that is within your power to do so that you don't feel so anxious about it? In which situations do you feel that your fear of crowds can be manageable? On the other hand, can you identify the situations where you feel that you cannot control your anxiety? By knowing these very important details, you will be able to manage your panic attacks and still function normally in society. Through your diary, you will be able to know a great deal about your condition. And as you learn more and more about yourself and your fear of crowds, you'll be able to help yourself overcome it. Remember that you are the master of yourself. With patience and determination, you will be able to get rid of this fear that's inhibiting you from living a fuller life.

Step 6: Seeking Professional Help

Enochlophobia is the irrational fear of crowds. A person suffering from this condition feels that he is in danger when in the midst of a large group of people, even when there is no reasonable cause for his anxiety. Many phobias develop in people during the childhood days and will persist until old age. However, there is no age limit for developing a phobia as it can be the result of a traumatic experience that might occur at any point in your life. So even teenagers, people in their 20's, middle-aged people, and even the elderly can still develop irrational fears of something.

There are a number of effective ways to overcome phobias. And certainly, there is no law preventing people from trying out efficient methods to help themselves get over a fear of something. Nevertheless, in the case of phobias, professional help is much needed. Phobias can escalate over time and without proper medical attention, the condition can debilitate a person. Enochlophobia is a very serious condition. It is the fear of facing a crowd, being in the midst of a crowd, interacting with a crowd. Social anxiety is just a factor contributing to enochlophobia. The condition involves so much more. For instance, an individual who has this fear can feel severely upset not only by the sight of large groups of people. He can also feel distressed about the smell, sound, feel, and movement of the crowd surrounding him.

Enochlophobia, is connected with so many other phobias, such as agoraphobia, which is the fear of open spaces, and claustrophobia which is the fear of closed spaces. A person who has enochlophobia, fear of crowds or groups of people, may feel anxious about riding an elevator or the subway train or some other closed space. At the same time, he can also feel panic attacks even when he is in open spaces like a baseball stadium, an outdoor concert, or even in a big mall.

The causes for developing encohlophobia can vary for each person and there is no sure method that can work for treating all people that suffer from it. One treatment may work for one patient, but this same method may not help another. Due to this fact, it is best to consult with a therapist, a professional who can help you overcome the fear of crowds. An expert on enochlophobia will work with the person suffering to identify specific root causes, and prescribe the most suitable type of treatment for the patient.

Here are some of the methods that a therapist can prescribe for people suffering from enochlophobia, the fear of crowds.

Medication

Your therapist can prescribe medication for severe panic attacks. In many cases, a person who has a fear of crowds can experience various symptoms such as:

- Headache
- Stomachache
- Blurry Vision
- Nausea
- Chest Pains Similar To Heart Attack
- Profuse sweating
- Fainting

These symptoms can cause real discomfort and inconvenience for people who have enochlophobia. In addition, when a person experiences these symptoms in public, he may become more scared about going out of his home, which can only contribute to making his fear of crowds even worse. The medications prescribed by the therapist will help keep panic attacks at bay and, at the same time, help control the advancement of enochlophobia.

Exposure Therapy

In this kind of therapy, the person suffering from a phobia is gradually exposed to the cause of his fear until the time he becomes more comfortable with the situation. The treatment has worked in dealing with various types of phobias. In the case of enochlophobia, the person suffering from it will gradually be placed in the presence of people, first in small groups and much later in bigger groups. For instance, Kay, who has been diagnosed with enochlophobia, is working with her therapist to overcome her fear of crowds. Through exposure therapy, she is now able to ride a subway train and even watch a concert without going into full-blown panic attacks.

The process of exposure therapy starts with creating a schedule for the patient during which he will be exposed to the stimuli causing his phobia and in the case of enochlophobia – crowds. The therapist and the patient will work out a schedule where the patient can go to a crowded place for limited periods. For example, the therapist will instruct the patient to just stand around the subway station for five minutes every day, with no intent of riding the train. After five minutes, he is instructed to leave and go home. After some time, the therapist can increase the time the patient is asked to stay in the subway station and even ask him to sit down and perhaps try to read a paper. This can go on until the patient feels comfortable doing this. Next, the therapist will ask the patient to attempt to ride the train but will remind him that it's okay not to do it in the event he feels any anxiety. The process of exposure therapy requires that it be done gradually so that the patient can react to the treatment more efficiently. The therapist can adjust the treatment according to how the patient reacts to it. The goal of exposure therapy is to make the person suffering from enochlophobia more and more comfortable in the presence of people. During the whole process, the patient can be asked to go to more crowded places, such as baseball games or concerts depending on his or her progress.

During the exercises, the patient can either go alone or with a family member to help him deal better with the situation. The family member can help the patient stay calm and at the same time, he can provide additional information about the whole experience. Oftentimes, the patient can report to the therapist about a perceived danger the family member has not seen. All these details can help in the recovery of the patient.

If you are wondering how long exposure therapy will take, the answer is that it all depends on the patient and the therapist. Although exposure therapy has produced good results for many, patients can and will experience setbacks. It is important to stay determined and not lose hope even when setbacks happen. Continue working with your therapist and with a positive mind, you can live a life that is free of this fear.

Hypnosis

Phobias are caused by various factors, but mostly by traumatic experiences. When people have traumatic experiences, the tendency is to bury unpleasant emotions. The emotional and mental shock are often not addressed because very few people seek treatment from a professional. It is better to just forget painful memories than to face it or relive the whole painful experience. In some cases, the person buries the unpleasant memory so deep in his mind that he totally forgets about it. He will have no memory of the event at all. As a result, it can be hard for the therapist to recommend treatment for a phobia if he does not know what caused it. Hypnosis is a type of treatment that therapists use in order to bring out repressed memories and emotions. If the enochlophobia was due to a traumatic past that has been repressed, then the therapist will need to bring it out so that proper treatment can be recommended and the healing process can finally begin.

Seeking the help of an expert is always necessary for any type of disorder, whether physical, emotional or mental. Before you jump into the conclusion that you do have enochlophobia or a fear of crowds, you need to be accurately diagnosed with it. The importance of correct diagnosis cannot be overemphasized. Never make the mistake of making a self-diagnosis based on your own readings, research, and conclusions. Always consult with a doctor for any event that you need help with your physical, emotional, and mental health.

Conclusion

While it may seem that the fear of crowds is a hopeless case, it really isn't. There are ways to overcome this phobia and it is possible to rejoin society once again. Any person suffering from a phobia will need the help of a skilled therapist. However, there are things that the person can do to help himself overcome this fear.

A lot of people suffering from phobias become a slave to their fear and allow their condition to take control of their lives. However, it does not need to be that way. Your life should not be limited just because of a fear. Fear of crowds can be the worst kind of phobia since man is naturally a social being. Being afraid of large groups of people is so unfortunate because it hinders the affected person from living his life to the fullest as he is not able to be in the presence of many people. This irrational fear will prevent him from sharing experiences with a crowd.

Humans are funny creatures and the mind of a human being is truly a powerful force to reckon. The mind can cause anyone to believe anything. Therefore, people with irrational fears need to, first and foremost, help themselves overcome their fear. The therapist is only there to guide and counsel the person through the healing process. In the end, it really is up to the person who has enochlophobia or any other type of phobia to fight his fear. Finally, it helps to keep your will strong and not allow your fears take control of you and your life. You are the master of your mind and the master of your life. Don't let your fear take over your life.

Finally, I'd like to thank you for purchasing this book! If you found it helpful, I'd greatly appreciate it if you'd take a moment to leave a review on Amazon. Thank you!

Printed in Great Britain
by Amazon